Monetary Mindfulness

for High School Students

ANSWER KEY

Dr. Angela K. Love

Angela K. Love
P.O. Box 452
Campbell TX 75422

Previously published December 2016 as *Personal Finance: A Working Textbook Solutions Manual.*
Previous published ISBN: 978-0-9978407-1-1

Cover design by Lisa Kerner at Designs by Lisa Kerner

Reach us on the Internet: www.angelakayelove.com

ISBN: 978-1-7342305-5-0

INTRODUCTION

This answer key is for the textbook, *Monetary Mindfulness for High School Students*, which is available for purchase separately. The textbook can be found where this answer key is sold.

ANSWER KEY

Section 1   Income and Expenses

Exercise 1.1

1. E
2. E
3. U
4. N
5. U
6. E
7. N
8. E
9. U
10. E

Exercise 1.2

1. b
2. d
3. f
4. e
5. a
6. c

Exercise 2

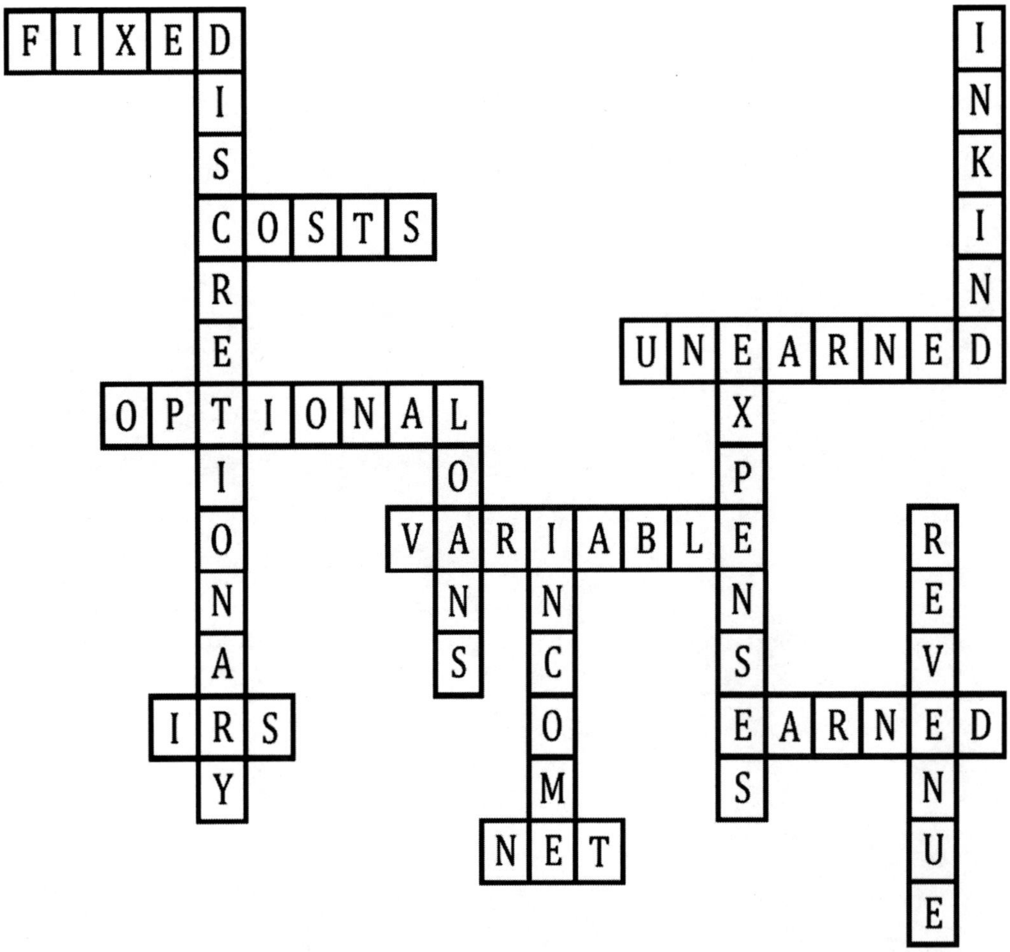

Across:

1. Fixed
2. Costs
3. Optional
4. IRS
5. Unearned
6. Variable
7. Net
8. Earned

Down:

9. Discretionary
10. Loans
11. Income
12. In-kind
13. Expenses
14. Revenue

Exercise 3.1

1. Savings
2. Answer can be any of the following:
   ... to purchase things in the future
   ... to use for investments
   ... to meet financial goals
   ... to pay expenses when needed
   ... to earn money
   ... for retirement.
3. Savings account
4. Share
5. Shareholders
6. Interest; interest rate
7. Dividends
8. Early withdrawal penalty
9. Loans
10. Liquid
11. Ladder
12. Future value
13. Calculator
14. Diversified

Exercise 3.2

1. .15%
2. 5 Years
3. $100,000
4. $50,000; $2,671.21 (52,671.21 – 50,000)

Exercise 4

1. False; Itemizing deductions is listing all allowable deductions in order to lower one's taxable income.
2. d – Freely giving something to someone without expecting anything in return.
3. True
4. 1040EZ
5. True
6. False; volunteering is good, but not deductible for tax purposes.
7. True
8. a; $4,400; receiving goods from a non-profit in exchange for money is not deductible.
9. True
10. True

Quiz - Section 1

1. False; Revenues is a term used by companies.
2. False; Fixed expenses are the same each month.
3. True
4. True
5. False; The IRS is the revenue service and tax collection agency for the Federal government.
6. True; Discretionary expenses are optional, variable expenses are necessary but can change.
7. False; Dividends are paid by a company to their shareholders.
8. False; giving is freely giving something to someone without an expectation of anything in return.
9. True
10. False; The maturity date on a loan is when the loan end.
11. b; interest earned from money in a CD is unearned income.
12. c
13. d
14. a; Giving is not receiving anything in return.
15. c
16. b
17. b; eating at a restaurant is optional.
18. d; Form 1040 is used for itemizing deductions, which includes charitable donations.
19. b
20. c
21. a; Liquid has to do with ease and accessibility
22. d
23. a
24. c
25. d

Section 2 Assets

Exercise 5.1

Answers will vary.

Exercise 5.2

1. c
2. f
3. d
4. g
5. b
6. a
7. e

Exercise 6

1. False; a short-term asset is an asset than can be sold, or converted to cash, within one year.
2. c
3. True
4. a
5. c; 12 months x $500 = $6,000
6. d; $500 x 5 months left on the loan = $2,500.
7. b; It becomes a short-term asset once maturity date is within one year.

Exercise 7

1. True
2. a; all of the other answers are examples of intangible assets.
3. d
4. c
5. True
6. b
7. False
8. d
9. b
10. True

Exercise 8

1. $4,250
2. $6,000
3. $30,000
4. $1,500
5. $2,000
6. $0
7. $105,000
8. $13,000
9. $28,000
10. $7,000
11. $196,750

Quiz - Section 2

1. False; accounts receivable is a current asset.
2. False; notes receivable is a noncurrent asset.
3. True
4. True
5. False; other terms for long-term assets are noncurrent and fixed assets.
6. False; a prepaid asset is when something is paid before it comes due.
7. True
8. True
9. True
10. False; PFS stands for Personal Financial Statement
11. a
12. c
13. b
14. d
15. $6,500
16. $11,000
17. $37,500
18. $2,500
19. $2,000
20. $0
21. $150,000
22. $10,000
23. $25,000
24. $14,900
25. $259,400

Section 3 Liabilities

Exercise 9

1. c
2. False; it is what is owed.
3. b
4. d
5. a
6. False; total assets should be greater than total debt.
7. False; total debt divided by total assets is the debt ratio formula.
8. b
9. True
10. True

Exercise 10

1. False; they are not recommended
2. False; a short-term liability is a debt obligation due within a year.
3. False; A PFS is for what is owed and owned.
4. True
5. True
6. True
7. c
8. b
9. a
10. d

Exercise 11

1. False; it is the remaining balance on a debt.
2. True
3. False; it's classified as a Mortgage on Real Estate.
4. False; it is a sign of poor financial health.
5. True
6. True
7. b
8. c
9. d
10. a

Exercise 12

1. $1,750
2. $9,900
3. $10,000
4. $0
5. $95,000
6. $0
7. $0
8. $116,650

Quiz - Section 3

1. c
2. b
3. a
4. c
5. b
6. $5,720
7. $9,500
8. $50,000
9. $1,500
10. $0
11. $5,000
12. $150,000
13. $14,550
14. $11,000
15. $0
16. $247,270
17. $2,300
18. $13,150
19. $12,500
20. $1,000
21. $124,589
22. $0
23. $0
24. $153,539
25. $93,731

Section 4 - Wages

Exercise 13

1. c
2. a
3. c

4. b
5. d
6. b
7. a
8. d
9. c
10. b; (20/2) + 20 = 30

Exercise 14

1. c
2. b
3. d
4. a
5. a
6. c
7. d
8. b
9. c
10. a

Exercise 15

1. c
2. d
3. a
4. a
5. d
6. b
7. d
8. c
9. a
10. b

Exercise 16

1. b; 15.00 x 80 = 1,200 and $22.50 (overtime pay) x 16 (overtime hours) = 360; 360+1,200 = $1,560
2. a
3. d
4. c
5. b

Quiz – Section 4

1. False
2. True
3. False
4. True
5. False
6. True
7. False
8. False
9. True
10. True
11. a
12. c
13. b
14. d
15. d
16. a
17. b
18. d
19. c
20. d
21. a
22. c
23. b
24. b
25. d

Section 5 - PFS

Exercise 17

1. Answer's will vary.
2. David Jones
3. 1234 Path Lane
4. Charleston, SC 29401
5. No answer
6. 843-555-1234
7. $2,700 (200 + 2,500)
8. $6,000
9. $0
10. $3,000
11. $0
12. $0
13. $0
14. $25,000 (17,000 + 8,000)
15. $5,000
16. $0
17. $41,700
18. $28,000

19. $0
20. $0
21. $0
22. $2,000
23. $12,000
24. $30,000
25. $0
26. $0
27. $0
28. $0
29. $44,000
30. $-2,300
31. $5,000
32. $0
33. $0

Exercise 18.1

1. February 27, 2016
2. David and Becky Jones
3. 5678 Holler Lane
4. Charleston, SC 29401
5. No answer
6. 843-555-7777
7. $1,800 (300 + 1,500)
8. $18,000 (12,000 + 6,000)
9. $80,000
10. $0
11. $20,000
12. $10,000
13. $150,000
14. $40,000 (22,000 + 9,000 + 9,000)
15. $41,000 (15,000 +20,000 + 6,000)
16. $0
17. $360,800
18. $98,000
19. $0
20. $0
21. $0
22. $8,000
23. $21,000 (6,000 + 15,000)
24. $0
25. $0
26. $112,500
27. $0
28. $0
29. $141,500
30. $219,300
31. $7,890
32. $0
33. $0

Exercise 18.2

Answers will vary, but should be along the lines of cashing in part of the stocks, using savings, using the CD money when it matures along with savings or stocks, or getting a loan on the life insurance cash value.

Exercise 19

1. Date will vary
2. David and Becky Jones
3. 5678 Holler Lane
4. Charleston, SC 29401
5. No answer
6. 843-555-7777
7. $3,700 (200 + 3,500)
8. $62,000 (20,000 + 42,000)
9. $500,000
10. $3,400
11. $32,000
12. $28,000
13. $230,000
14. $72,000 (15,000 + 12,000 + 45,000)
15. $90,000 (25,000 +35000 + 30,000)
16. $0
17. $1,021,100
18. $170,000
19. $0
20. $0
21. $18,000
22. $0
23. $20,000
24. $0
25. $0
26. $0
27. $0

28. $0
29. $20,000
30. $1,001,100
31. $0
32. $0
33. $0

Quiz – Section 5

1. False
2. True
3. True
4. True
5. True
6. False
7. False
8. False
9. True
10. False

Unit I Test

1. b
2. a
3. b
4. c
5. a
6. d
7. c
8. a
9. c
10. b
11. d
12. a
13. c
14. b
15. d
16. c
17. a
18. a
19. c
20. b
21. d
22. a
23. b
24. c
25. d
26. a
27. b
28. c
29. d
30. b
31. a
32. c
33. a
34. b
35. d

Exercise 20

1. c
2. d
3. a
4. a
5. b

Exercise 21

1. b
2. a
3. d
4. c
5. b; 10,000 x .055 x 15 = $18,250

For the answers for Questions 6-10, the letter represents the answer if the recommended online calculator is used. If the student uses a scientific calculator, the letter is still the closest answer, but the calculation and exact answer is shown below.

6. b; Using a scientific calculator:

FV = 4,000 (1 + .07/1)25(1)
FV = 4,000 (1 + 0.07)25(1)
FV = 4,000 (1.07)25(11)
FV = 4,000 (1.07)25
FV = 21,709.73

7. d; Using a scientific calculator:

FV = 4,000 (1 + .07/12)25(12)
FV = 4,000 (1 + 0.0058)25(12)
FV = 4,000 (1.0058)25(12)
FV = 4,000 (1.0058)300
FV = 22,675.11

8. a; Using a scientific calculator:

FV = 23,000 (1 + .05/1)20(1)
FV = 23,000 (1 + 0.05)20(1)
FV = 23,000 (1.05)20(1)
FV = 23,000 (1.05)20
FV = 61,025.85

9. c; Using a scientific calculator:

FV = 23,000 (1 + .05/12)20(12)
FV = 23,000 (1 + 0.0042)20(12)
FV = 23,000 (1.0042)20(12)
FV = 23,000 (1.0042)240
FV = 62,889.76

10. b; Using a scientific calculator:

FV = 7,000 (1 + .06/12)40(12)
FV = 7,000 (1 + 0.005)40(12)
FV = 7,000 (1.005)40(12)
FV = 7,000 (1.005)480
FV = 76,702.18

Exercise 22

1. False
2. True
3. True
4. False
5. True
6. False
7. False
8. True
9. True
10. False

Exercise 23

1. False
2. False
3. True
4. False
5. True
6. b
7. c
8. d
9. a
10. b

Quiz – Section 6

1. True
2. True
3. False
4. False
5. True
6. True
7. False
8. True
9. True
10. False
11. c
12. d
13. b
14. a

For the answers for Questions 15-18, the letter represents the answer if the recommended online calculator is used. If the student uses a scientific calculator, the letter is still the closest answer, but the calculation and exact answer is shown below.

15. b; Using a scientific calculator:

FV = 8,000 (1 + .08/1)30(1)
FV = 8,000 (1 + 0.08)30(1)
FV = 8,000 (1.08)30(1)
FV = 8,000 (1.08)30
FV = 80,501.26

16. d; Using a scientific calculator:

FV = 9,000 (1 + .06/12)30(12)
FV = 9,000 (1 + 0.005)30(12)
FV = 9,000 (1.005)30(12)
FV = 9,000 (1.005)360
FV = 54,203.18

17. c; Using a scientific calculator:

FV = 2,000 (1 + .06/12)20(12)
FV = 2,000 (1 + 0.005)20(12)
FV = 2,000 (1.005)20(12)
FV = 2,000 (1.005)240
FV = 6,620.41

18. b; Using a scientific calculator:

FV = 15,000 (1 + .05/1)40(1)
FV = 15,000 (1 + 0.05)40(1)
FV = 15,000 (1.05)40(1)
FV = 15,000 (1.05)40
FV = 105,599.83

19. a
20. c

Exercise 24

1. Credit unions
2. Savings, loans
3. Commercial banks
4. Field, membership
5. Stockholders or shareholders
6. Savings and loans
7. Members, rates, fees – or – members, fees, rates
8. Profit, operations
9. Mutual ownership model
10. Non-profit

Exercise 25

1. May 11,2013
2. Swimsuits R Us
3. Thirty-eight and 56/100 -------------
4. 38.56
5. Swimsuit for vacation
6. Jessica Smith
7. c
8. a
9. d
10. c

Exercise 26

1. True
2. False
3. True
4. True
5. False; the NCUA insures credit unions
6. True
7. False; $250,000
8. True
9. False
10. True

Exercise 27

The completed register for problems 1 – 10 should look like the illustration on the next page. A student may use other terminology when defining a transaction such as using "eating out" for "dining," which is okay to do. Names of payees, dates, REF, and transaction amounts should be completed according the solution illustration on the next page.

DATE	REF	DESCRIPTION OF TRANSACTION	PAYMENT / DEBIT (-)	R	C	DEPOSIT / CREDIT (+)	BALANCE
10/1/2013		Beginning Balance			✓		200.00
10/3/2013	DEBIT	Walmart Groceries	86.46		✓		113.54
10/5/2013	461	Municipal Water Company Water bill	43.98		✓		69.56
10/8/2013	DEBIT	Qdoba Dining or dining with friends	10.43		✓		59.13
10/12/2013	ATM	Cash withdrawal Miscellaneous or no answer here	20.00		✓		39.13
10/15/2013	DEP	Paycheck			✓	764.26	803.39
10/16/2013	462	Lakewood Apartments Rent or rent payment	400.00				403.39
10/18/2013	DEBIT	Flying J Fuel or gas	29.13				374.26
10/20/2013	DEBIT	JC Penneys Clothing	26.46				347.80

Exercise 28

Error 1 – Walmart should be $98.37 in the checkbook register.

Error 2 – The check number for the Power Company should be 947.

Error 3 – The purchase at the Movie Theater needs to be entered into the checkbook register.

Quiz – Section 7

The completed register for problems 1 – 10 should look like the illustration below.

DATE	REF	DESCRIPTION OF TRANSACTION	PAYMENT / DEBIT (-)	R	C	DEPOSIT / CREDIT (+)	BALANCE
6/20/2015		Beginning Balance			✓		300.00
7/1/2015	DEP	Paycheck			✓	1,263.89	1,563.89
7/1/2015	724	Westlake Apartments Rent	600.00		✓		963.89
7/3/2015	DEBIT	Safeway Groceries	136.45		✓		827.44
7/4/2015	ATM	Cash withdrawal Entertainment	40.00		✓		787.44
7/11/2015	DEP	Check Reimbursement for Mark			✓	50.00	837.44
7/15/2015	725	Verizon Cell phone bill	60.53				776.91
7/15/2015	DEBIT	Conoco Fuel or gas	35.46				741.45
7/17/2015	DEBIT	McDonald's Dining with friends	9.27				732.18

11. b
12. a
13. c
14. a
15. d
16. b
17. c
18. b
19. d
20. a
21. d
22. c
23. b
24. a
25. d

Exercise 29

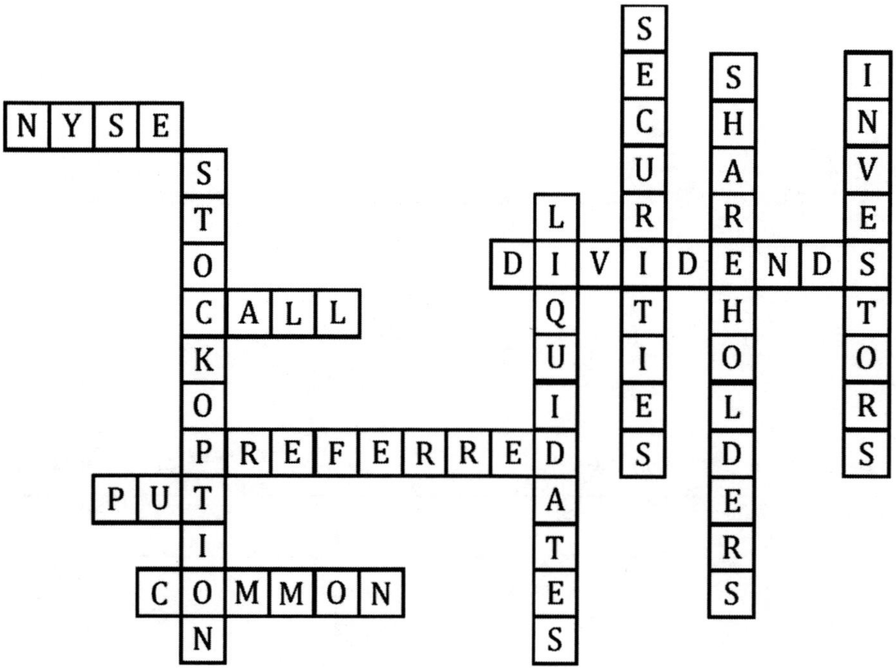

Across

1. NYSE
3. CALL
4. PREFERRED
5. PUT
6. COMMON
8. DIVIDENDS

Down

2. STOCK OPTION
7. LIQUIDATES
9. SECURITIES
10. SHAREHOLDERS
11. INVESTORS

Exercise 30

1. b
2. a
3. b
4. c
5. d
6. a
7. c
8. b
9. d
10. c

Exercise 31

1. e
2. h
3. f
4. d
5. g

6. c
7. a
8. b

Exercise 32

1. False; Passive income is earned by not actively participating.
2. True
3. True
4. False; Mailbox money is passive income.
5. True
6. True
7. True
8. False; investments should be diversified
9. True
10. False

Quiz – Section 8

1. a
2. b
3. c
4. b
5. d
6. c
7. a
8. c
9. d
10. b
11. c
12. a
13. a
14. d
15. b
16. c
17. d
18. b
19. a
20. b
21. c
22. d
23. c
24. a
25. b

Exercise 33

1. b
2. b
3. c
4. a
5. d
6. c
7. a
8. b
9. d
10. d

Exercise 34

1. c
2. b
3. a
4. b
5. c
6. a
7. b
8. b
9. d
10. c

Exercise 35

For the answers for Questions 1-5, the letter represents the answer if the recommended online calculator is used. If the student uses a scientific calculator, the letter is still the closest answer, but the calculation and exact answer is shown below.

1. a; Using a scientific calculator:

PMT = 4,000(0.03/12) / 1-(1+0.03/12)-36
PMT = 10 / 1-(1.0025)-36
PMT = 10 / 1-(0.9140)
PMT = 10 / 0.086
PMT = 116.28

2. c; If using a scientific calculator:

PMT = 9,000(0.04/12) /
1-(1+0.04/12)-48
PMT = 30 / 1-(1.0033)-48
PMT = 30 / 1-(0.8537)
PMT = 30 / 0.1463
PMT = $205.06

3. c; If using a scientific calculator:

PMT = 17,000(.05/12) /
1-(1+.05/12)-60
PMT = 70.83 / 1-(1.00417)-60
PMT = 70.83 / 1-(0.7791)
PMT = 70.83 / 0.2209
PMT = $320.64

4. b; Using a scientific calculator:

PMT = 60,000(.07/12) /
1-(1+.07/12)-120
PMT = 350 / 1-(1.0058)-120
PMT = 350 / 1-(0.4996)
PMT = 350 / 0.5004
PMT = $699.44

5. a; Using a scientific calculator:

PMT = 120,000(.06/12) /
1-(1+.06/12)-180
PMT = 600 / 1-(1.005)-180
PMT = 600 / 1-(0.4075)
PMT = 600 / 0.5925
PMT = $1,012.66

Quiz – Section 9

For the answers for Questions 3, 6, 9, 12, and 15, the letter represents the answer if the recommended online calculator is used. If the student uses a scientific calculator, the letter is still the closest answer, but the calculation and exact answer is shown below.

1. c
2. a
3. b; Using a scientific calculator:

PMT = 6,000(.03/12) /
1-(1+.03/12)-36
PMT = 15 / 1-(1.0025)-36
PMT = 15 / 1-(0.9140)
PMT = 15 / 0.086
PMT = $174.42

4. b
5. d
6. a; Using a scientific calculator:

PMT = 76,000(.05/12) /
1-(1+.05/12)-120
PMT = 316.67 / 1-(1.0042)-120
PMT = 316.67 / 1-(0.6048)
PMT = 316.67 / 0.3952
PMT = $801.29

7. d
8. c
9. b; Using a scientific calculator:

PMT = 11,000(.02/12) /
1-(1+.02/12)-48
PMT = 18.33 / 1-(1.0017)-48
PMT = 18.33 / 1-(0.9217)
PMT = 18.33 / 0.0783
PMT = $234.10

10. d
11. a
12. d; Using a scientific calculator:

PMT = 16,000(.0250/12) /
1-(1+.0250/12)-60
PMT = 33.33 / 1-(1.0021)-60
PMT = 33.33 / 1-(0.8817)
PMT = 33.33 / 0.1183
PMT = $281.74

13. c
14. b
15. c; Using a scientific calculator:

PMT = 23,000(.0325/12) /
1-(1+.0325/12)-72
PMT = 62.29 / 1-(1.0027)-72
PMT = 62.29 / 1-(0.8235)
PMT = 62.29 / 0.1765
PMT = $352.92

Exercise 36

1. a
2. c
3. b
4. d
5. c
6. c; 1,400 / 4,600 = 30.44%
7. b; 1,000 / 3,300 = 30.30%
8. a; 750 / 2,400 = 31.25%
9. d; 832 / 1,400 = 59.43%
10. a; 800 / 1,629 = 49.11%

Exercise 37

1. credit report
2. Experian, Equifax, TransUnion (in any order)
3. character
4. denied
5. will not
6. free; once
7. discrepancy or error; dispute
8. FICO
9. 45
10. list

Exercise 38

1. a
2. c
3. d
4. b
5. b
6. c
7. b
8. a
9. c
10. d

Quiz – Section 10

1. b
2. a
3. b
4. c
5. d
6. c
7. a
8. b
9. b
10. d
11. a
12. c
13. a
14. d
15. b

Unit II Test

For the answers for Questions 11, 27, and 34, the letter represents the answer if the recommended online calculator is used. If the student uses a scientific calculator, the letter is still the closest answer, but the calculation and exact answer is shown below.

1. a
2. c
3. b
4. b
5. d
6. a
7. c
8. c
9. b
10. d
11. a; Using a scientific calculator:

    $PMT = 46{,}000(0.06/12) / 1\text{-}(1+0.06/12)\text{-}84$

    $PMT = 230 / 1\text{-}(1.005)\text{-}84$

    $PMT = 230 / 1\text{-}(0.6577)$

    $PMT = 230 / 0.3423$

    $PMT = 671.93$
12. b
13. c
14. d
15. a
16. c
17. d
18. b
19. a
20. b
21. c
22. d

23. b
24. b
25. a
26. d
27. c; Using a scientific calculator:

    PMT =6,200(0.04/12) /
    1-(1+0.04/12)-36
    PMT = 20.67 / 1-(1.0033)-36
    PMT = 20.67 / 1-(0.8882)
    PMT = 20.67 / 0.1118
    PMT = 184.88
28. d; (550+68+160+175) / 1,543
29. b
30. c
31. c
32. a
33. b
34. c; Using a scientific calculator:
    FV = 7,000 (1 + .05/12)10(12)
    FV = 7,000 (1+ 0.0042)10(12)
    FV = 7,000 (1.0042)120
    FV = 11,575.08
35. d

Exercise 39

Answers will vary for this exercise.

Exercise 40.1

The list can be in any order, but should contain these ten items. The student can refer back to the lesson as they complete the exercise.

1. Don’t use credit cards as a source of cash.
2. Always put a percentage of each paycheck into savings.
3. Plan for fun!
4. Learn to say “no” to wants...plan for them instead.
5. Don’t borrow to the maximum limit available.
6. Remember! Debt doesn’t increase wealth!
7. Live within the parameters of the paycheck.
8. Always have a healthy cushion between total monthly expenses and payments and total net income.
9. Be a continual learner of finance.
10. Create a budget and follow it; adjusting when necessary.

Exercise 40.2

Answers will vary, but should be focused on not incurring debt and ways to decrease expenses.

Exercise 41

1. True
2. False
3. True
4. True
5. Answers will vary.
6. Answers will vary.
7. Answers will vary.
8. Answers will vary.

Exercise 42

1. False
2. True
3. True
4. False
5. True
6. True
7. False
8. False
9. True
10. True

There is no Quiz for Sections 11 and 12. This is intentional since the exercises are more personal and subjective in nature.

Exercise 43

1. list expected expenses and income for a given time period

2. adjust expenses so there is not a deficit

3. follow the created budget
4. make adjustments to the budget as necessary
5. c
6. b
7. a
8. c
9. d
10. b

Exercise 44

1. 1,800.00
2. 0
3. 0
4. 0
5. 1,800.00
6. 180.00
7. 25.00
8. 350.00
9. 25.00
10. 195.00
11. 120.00
12. 25.99
13. 225.00
14. 73.15
15. 75.20
16. 46.29
17. 30.82
18. 0
19. 0
20. 144.82
21. 20.37
22. 22.22
23. 62.75
24. 125.59
25. 1,747.20
26. 52.80

Exercise 45

1. True
2. True
3. True
4. True
5. True
6. True
7. True
8. True
9. True
10. True

Exercise 46

Answers will vary.

Final Comprehensive Exam

1. b
2. a
3. d
4. b
5. c
6. a
7. a
8. b
9. b
10. c
11. a
12. d
13. b
14. c
15. d
16. a
17. b
18. c
19. b
20. d
21. a
22. c
23. c
24. a
25. c
26. b
27. c
28. a
29. d
30. c
31. d
32. d
33. a
34. b
35. c
36. b
37. d
38. c

39. d
40. b
41. c
42. b
43. b
44. c
45. a
46. b
47. c
48. b
49. c
50. a

Made in United States
Cleveland, OH
05 November 2026

47664971R00019